I would like to dedicate this book to my wife, Sandy, and my children, Sara and Andy. And to thank God for all the wonderful blessings he has granted us.

Thank you also to all my friends, co-workers, and colleagues who have contributed to the success of this book.

Special thanks to Michael Toth for his direction, Denise Dennison for typing, Mindy Wygonik for editing skills and to Diane Staszkiewicz for her creative designs.

Photography by Frank Olma.

BIOGRAPHY

❖

ALBERT WUTSCH, director of Indiana University of Pennsylvania Academy of Culinary Arts, is a certified executive chef and culinary educator who combines his mastery of cooking with his passion for the great outdoors.

An avid hunter and outdoorsman, Chef Wutsch has cooked for professional outfitters in Montana's Bob Marshall, Scapegoat and Spotted Bear Wilderness, the largest untamed areas in America. He has cooked in many hunting camps throughout the country and has taught courses on game cookery in Montana, Florida, Pennsylvania, and New Jersey. He has been a featured guest speaker for many sports shows including the Eastern Sports and Outdoor Show, the largest outdoor show in North America.

Chef Wutsch's professional career has spanned over 25 years of culinary experience. He has received numerous culinary teaching awards, and has been the subject of featured newspaper articles as well as radio and TV interviews. Chef Wutsch has judged competitions and has been retained by publishers to review culinary manuscripts. He has owned and operated a catering business in Montana and has specialized in catering throughout the country including upscale events in Palm Beach Florida.

He is owner of Cache Creek Enterprises that includes mail-order specialty items, and a game recipe booklet and he is currently developing videos, and a game cookbook series. Cache Creek also recruits employment opportunities and placement of chefs and cooks for camps and outfitters. Chef Wutsch is available by request for special events, cooking demonstrations, speaking engagements, seminars, hunting and fishing camp chef, and consulting. See booking procedures on *Cache Creek Enterprises Information Page.*

TABLE OF CONTENTS

❖

FORWARD

❖

Venison is a healthy, low fat, low cholesterol, red meat, robust in flavor and easily accessible. Too often, venison is improperly prepared and thus not fully enjoyed. There are many factors that affect taste and tenderness including age, type of feed, habitat, how the animal was shot, field dressed and transported. Temperature has a major effect on processing. However, the most important element in maintaining tenderness and taste is what you do at the stove. A good cook can start with a tough piece of meat and finish with a masterpiece.

The Art of Cooking Venison is a recipe book emphasizing cooking methods and techniques revealing the chef's secrets. The recipes in this book use the term *venison* but can be interchangeable with any of the game animals classified under the Deer family including Moose, Elk, Caribou, Antelope and all variations of deer.

The section on *Field Care* is essential to making the meat palatable and determining wholesomeness. It covers procedures and techniques used for safety and sanitation.

Nutritional Information based on the USDA research—venison analysis by the National Food Laboratory, Inc. It is a comparison of venison to other forms of meats.

The Butchery (Fabrication) section identifies where the tender and less tender cuts are located on the animal. It is these cuts that will determine the best cooking method.

The Recipes are classified by cooking method for your convenience. Each section contains cooking tips and important procedures. Recipes are guidelines, so please make notes as you go, try them and adjust them to your individual tastes.

The *Glossary of Cooking Terms, Measures and Safe Cooking Tips* defines culinary terms, methods and techniques with emphasis on safety procedures and key points in maintaining wholesomeness. Chef Wutsch's mailing address, e-mail address, web page, and booking procedures are located on the *Cache Creek Enterprises Informational Page.*

Field Care

The most important step of field care is to lower the animal's body temperature. The animal needs to be cooled as fast as possible. Clean the entrails and open the body cavity to air. Do not pack with snow. Snow works as an insulator and prevents the heat from escaping.

The second most important step is the bleeding of the carcass. Simply clean and then hang the animal with its head down. Do not cut the animal's throat once it is dead, since this will ruin both the meat and the cape.

The meat will age by hanging. The best temperature range for tenderness and safety is 35-45°F. for approximately 3 to 5 days. Aging increases tenderness and flavor. If the temperature outside is too warm, skin the deer and cut into large pieces (primal cuts) and place in the refrigerator.

The big question is: Do I skin the animal or leave the hide on? Such circumstances as the weather, transportation, time and skill will all be determining factors. Skinning is a personal choice. The skin comes off easier when the animal is still warm; but on the other hand, when the hide is left on, there is less drying of the outer surface and less waste. Some outdoorsmen say the skin taints the meat; this is debatable.

Be careful not to touch the scent glands when handling and touching the meat. Also, try not to cut the bladder or the stomach when field dressing, but most importantly, remove all blood and bloodshot meat. Keep the meat clean and free of debris. These basic steps are integral to the quality, wholesomeness, tenderness and taste of the finished product.

NUTRITIONAL INFORMATION

Venison is a healthy choice and a new alternative for other red meats. It is low fat, low cholesterol, high protein and low calories without chemical additives. Venison is very popular in today's professional circuit, promoting health and foods indigenous to America. It is the main thrust for developing American Cuisine. The table below is a comparison of nutritional values.

Comparative Nutritional Table:

Calories, cholesterol, fat, and protein content of various types of meat (3-ounce cooked portions).

Meat types	Calories	Cholesterol (MG)	Fat (MG)	Protein (MG)
Venison Loin	139	62	5	22
Beef brisket	223	77	13	24
Ground beef	213	84	12	25
Pork shoulder	207	82	13	22
Beef bottom round	189	81	8	27
Lamb loin	183	80	8	25
Veal cutlet	155	112	4	28
Chicken breast	140	72	3	26
Salmon	140	60	5	22

Source: USDA research— venison analysis by The National Food Laboratory, Inc.

VENISON BUTCHERY OR FABRICATION

There are many ways to **BUTCHER** or process your deer. Most people take their game to a processing house and ask for steaks from the hind leg, chops from the loin, and ground meat from whatever remains. This limits your ability to create special dishes like crown roasts, whole leg roasts, or rack of venison, etc.

Ask your butcher for specific cuts or grinds, like a coarse grind for chili or a whole hind leg for a Super Bowl Sunday BBQ. (If you are on good terms with your butcher, he will be able to supply all the cuts used in this book and any other cuts associated with beef, veal and pork.) If unsure of what to have processed, ask for the hind leg to be processed into muscle roasts. This is a safe way to store your meat, and the uses are endless.

When choosing a game processor, check around by asking for references. Some processors have a bad reputation, and you may not get the meat you brought in. There are many selections of processed meats available such as jerky and an endless variety of sausages.

There are many factors in the field that determine how you should butcher your game. Temperature is the number one factor, while others would include transportation, storage, and skill level of the meat cutter.

If you choose to fabricate the animal yourself, refer to Cache Creek Enterprise's video series. This information is located on the *Cache Creek Informational Page*.

VENISON Primal Cuts

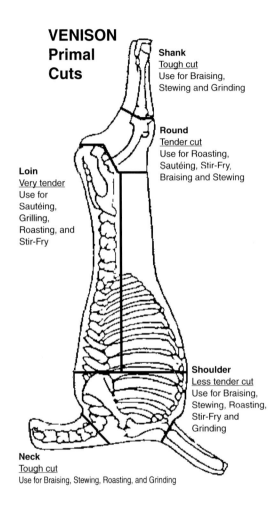

Shank
Tough cut
Use for Braising,
Stewing and Grinding

Round
Tender cut
Use for Roasting,
Sautéing, Stir-Fry,
Braising and Stewing

Loin
Very tender
Use for
Sautéing,
Grilling,
Roasting, and
Stir-Fry

Shoulder
Less tender cut
Use for Braising,
Stewing, Roasting,
Stir-Fry and
Grinding

Neck
Tough cut
Use for Braising, Stewing, Roasting, and Grinding

Venison Butchery
Cuts

❖

Chops: Cut from the loin, bone-in or boneless. Usually 1-inch thick round cuts.

Medallions: From the loin or round, boneless $\frac{1}{8}$-to $\frac{1}{2}$-inch thick, 2-inch round sliver dollar shaped.

Strips: Cut from the loin, round or even off the shoulder. Small $\frac{1}{2}$-inch wide, $\frac{1}{4}$-inch thick, 1 to 2 inches long.

Butterfly: To slice a piece of meat 3/4 of the way through from the side, opening the two halves into wings like a butterfly. This can be done with chops, medallions, round steaks and even the neck.

Cubes: Usually cut from the round, shank, neck or other scrap meats. A 1/2-inch square is good for faster cooking and small enough to prevent choking.

Cube Steaks: Come from the round or shoulder and processed through a cuber (tenderizing machine).

Roasts: Cuts from almost any part of the animal. Usually cut by seaming the muscle into sections. Size ranges from a two-pound boneless roast to a bone-in whole leg roast.

Grinding: This meat should be clean and free of hair, bloodshot and heavy sinew. You can grind it coarsely or fine depending upon its use. Some people prefer to mix it with pork for a moister product.

Shopping List For Your Butcher
of Selected Cuts

❖

Shank Tough cut, used for braising, stewing, and grinding.
- Boneless/bone-in
- Cube
- Ground

Round Tender cut, used for roasting, sautéing , braising, stewing, and stir-fry.
- Roasts
- Whole leg roast
- Medallions
- Cubes
- Strips
- Butterfly steaks

Loin Very Tender, used for sautéing, grilling, roasting, and stir-fry.
- Roasts
- Medallions
- Butterfly steaks
- Strips
- Chops
- Rack of venison from the rib

Shoulder Less tender cut, used for braising, stewing, roasting, and stir-fry.
- Roasts
- Medallions
- Strips
- Cubes
- Ground
- Butterfly

Neck Tough cut, used for braising, stewing, roasting or grinding.
- Roasts
- Cubes
- Ground
- Butterfly

Glossary of Cooking Terms and Measurements

❖

Cooking Terms

Blanch: To cook an item briefly in boiling water or hot fat before finishing or storing it.

Caramelizing or **searing:** To brown the meat on both sides—browning enhances color, taste and tenderness. When caramelizing meat, do not overload the pan. This will lower the temperature and sweat the meat, making the product tough, colorless and tasteless.

Concasser: A skinless, seedless, rough chopped tomato.

Deglazing: To add liquid to the pan to remove the fond (browned juices that have stuck to the bottom of the pan). Also adds flavor and color.

Dredge: To coat food with a dry or moist ingredient such as flour, bread crumbs, spices, or oil.

Flambé: To describe food that is ignited with a small amount of heated liquor poured over it, the burning alcohol enveloping the dish in flames. A note of caution: pour the liquor into a glass or cup, then pour into the heated pan. Pouring directly from the bottle can create a fire hazard.

Larding: To insert fat, and **Barding** means to cover with fat in order to add moisture and flavor.

Marinate: To place meat in an acid and herbs to tenderize and flavor.

Pan Roasting: Browning the meat in a hot pan on the stove, then finishing in the oven at 375°F.

Reserve: To keep back or save for future use or a special purpose.

Shock: Placing pasta or vegetables under cold running water to stop the cooking process. This will also retain color and crispness.

Measurements

c = cup	qt = quart
T = Tablespoon	oz = ounce
tsp = teaspoon	

Safe Cooking Tips

❖

- Keep meat cold at all times.
- Use clean equipment.
- When in doubt, throw it out.
- Keep hot foods hot and cold foods cold.
- Wash your hands.
- Double wrap meats for freezing.
- Do not use bloodshot meat.
- Use sharp knives.
- Always cut away from yourself.
- Use latex gloves when field dressing game.
- Remove all hair.
- Use 3 parts fresh herbs to every 1 part dry herbs.
- The tender cuts can be broiled, sautéed, roasted and stir-fried.
- Tough cuts should be roasted, braised, stewed or ground.
- Always cut meat across the grain. This will aide in tenderness.
- Remove the silverskin that covers most muscles. Also remove the thin sticky membrane that covers the meat. This will eliminate the gamy taste, lower the cholesterol level and prevent the meat from twisting (contorting) out of shape during cooking.
- Cook meats rare (140°F, internal temperature), for the most tender product. When cooked well-done, all moisture is lost giving you a tough product.

Broiling, Grilling, and Barbecuing are all dry heat cooking methods and the most popular used today. In broiling, the heat source comes from above such as a commercial broiler or a broiling unit in a house-hold stove. Grilling means the heat source comes from below such as a grill or barbecue unit. Barbecuing is the same as grilling only applying lower temperatures and taking more time. Barbecuing, usually, uses a sauce made of an acid or sugar base.

- Always use tender cuts of meat from the loin or round.
- Preheat the grill—smoking hot— this will sear the meat and prevent it from sticking.
- Dredge (coat) the meat in seasoned oil or spice blends.
- Keep the grill clean so foods will not stick.
- Use marinades to tenderize and flavor.
- Turn once. The more you turn the meat, the tougher it will become.
- Cover to retain heat.
- Serve with sauces, flavored butters, chutney, salsa or glazes.

CIDER VENISON RIBS WITH APPLE BBQ SAUCE

Venison ribs, 2 racks

Marinade:

Liquid smoke 1 T
Apple cider 1 pt

Sauce:

Oil 1 t
Onion, finely chopped 1 c
Apple cider 1 c
Soy sauce ¼ c
Ketchup ½ c
Honey ½ c
Apple jelly ¼ c

Cornstarch 1 T
Apple cider ¼ c

Remove skin on inside of ribs and marinate for two days. In a saucepan, sauté onion and add remaining sauce ingredients. Mix cornstarch with apple cider, then add to sauce and cook until thick. Glaze ribs with sauce while grilling.

Yields: 2 servings

VENISON SATE WITH PEANUT SAUCE

Venison, 2 lb. (sliced across the grain)
into ⅛" thick, 1" wide, 2" long pieces

Marinade:

Ginger, minced 1 T
Garlic, minced ¼ c
Sesame oil 2 T
Brown sugar ½ c
Soy sauce ½ c
Ketchup ¼ c

Peanut Sauce:

Sesame oil 2 T
Garlic, chopped 1 T
Ginger, chopped 1 T
Cayenne pepper ½ tsp.
Rice wine vinegar ¼ c
Honey ¼ c
Chunky peanut butter ½ c
Soy sauce to taste

Bamboo skewers

Marinate meat 1-2 hours. Prepare the peanut sauce by sautéing the garlic and ginger. Add cayenne and remaining ingredients, and simmer for 15 minutes. Place meat on bamboo skewers, grill, and serve with peanut dipping sauce. Note: soak the bamboo skewers overnight to prevent burning.

Yields: 6 servings

GRILLED VENISON ROUND WITH PORTABELLO MUSHROOMS

Venison, 2 lbs (bottom round leg roast)
Portabello mushrooms, 6 ea

Marinade:

Catalina French dressing 1 qt
Sherry wine 1 pt

Marinate meat and mushrooms overnight. Grill meat and mushrooms. Serve with grilled corn and tomatoes. Boil the marinade and serve as sauce.

Yields: 6 servings

TERIYAKI VENISON SKEWERS

*Venison 2 lbs (sliced across the grain)
into ⅛" thick, 1" wide, 2" long pieces*

Marinade:

*Ginger, minced 1 T
Garlic, minced 2 T
Green onion, chopped ¼ c
Sesame oil 2 T
Sherry wine ¼ c
Teriyaki sauce ½ c
Hoisin sauce 2 T*

Bamboo skewers

Marinate meat 1-2 hours. Place meat on bamboo skewers, and grill.

Serve as an appetizer or with Chinese steamed vegetables and rice.

Note: soak the bamboo skewers overnight to prevent burning.

Yields: 6 servings

STOCKMAN'S COFFEE JERKY

Venison, 1 lb (sliced thin with the grain)
into ¼" thick, 1" wide, 3-4" long pieces

Ingredients:

Salt 1 tsp
Kahlúa ½ c
Brown sugar 1 T

Combine salt and brown sugar with kahlúa. Add meat and toss.
Marinate 1-2 hours. Dry in oven (150°F) until dry but not completely
brittle. You may also use a dehydrator, smokehouse grill or barbecuing
unit. The best way to store dry jerky is to freeze in air tight bags.

Yields: Approximately 4 ounces dried

ROASTING

Everyone loves the aroma of roasting meats. This popular dry heat cooking method uses an oven setting of approximately 350-400°F. These key points will ensure a tasty, tender outstanding feast.

- Use tender or less tender cuts from the loin or the round.
- Use larger pieces, approximately 2 pounds or larger, for roasting.
- Bard or lard the meat. This means either wrap, cover or insert fat such as wrapping a steak with bacon, placing bacon on top of a roast or inserting fat with a larding needle. This adds flavor and moisture to the meat.
- Roast the meat on a rack or bed of vegetables.
- Tie with string to maintain shape.
- Season (rub) the outside with spices or spice blends.
- Roast with high heat to start the browning process (caramelization), 400°F then finish with low heat of 300-350°F.
- Always cook rare, remove from the oven at 125-130°F internal temperature.
- After roasting, wrap in foil and let rest 20 minutes. This will carry the internal temperature up to 140°F as well as let the juices redistribute throughout the meat.
- Baste the meat with the marinade, broth, wine or water. This will also help keep the meat moist.
- Add liquid for gravy by removing the browned juices from the pan (deglazing).
- Always roast in a pan where the sides are lower than the meat. This will allow proper browning. Otherwise the meat steams and prevents browning, making it tough and rubbery.

ROAST LOIN OF VENISON
RUBBED WITH FRESH SAGE AND THYME

Venison, loin 1 lb

Marinade:

Olive oil ¼ c
Fresh sage, chopped 2 T
Fresh thyme, chopped 1 T
Salt
White pepper

Sauce:

Garlic, chopped 1T
Whole peeled tomatoes, sliced 1 pt
Fresh sage, chopped 1 T
Fresh thyme, chopped 1 T

Marinate the loin for 2 hours. Pan roast the loin by browning the meat in a hot pan on the stove, then finishing in the oven at 375°F for approximately 15 to 20 minutes. In a 2 qt saucepan, sauté the garlic, then add the tomatoes and herbs. Bring to a boil and reduce until thick. Place seasoned tomatoes on a platter and top with the roast. Slice to order. Remember to serve meat rare. Well-done meat will be tough because of the loss of juices.

Yields: 4 servings

Stuffed Loin of Venison with Spinach and Fennel

Venison, loin 2 lbs
Olive oil 2 T
Salt and white pepper to taste

Ingredients:

Onions ¼ c
Fresh spinach 12 oz bag
Fennel seed, crushed 1 tsp
Fresh cracked black pepper 1 tsp
Salt to taste
White bread, cut into small dice 1 slice

Sauce:

Brown sauce 1 pt

Butterfly the loin and season with salt, pepper, and oil. Remove stems from spinach and blanch in boiling water. Shock in cold water to maintain bright green. Drain well and squeeze out most of the water. Reserve. Sauté onions, fennel, and pepper. Add bread and let cool. Combine spinach and onion mixture and place inside the loin. Roll and tie closed. Use toothpicks—just be sure to remove before serving. In a sauté pan on the stove top, brown the meat in oil. Place on rack and roast for approximately 30 minutes or until internal temperature reaches 135°F. Let rest for 15 minutes and slice into ½-inch thick slices. Serve with brown sauce and fresh roasted tomatoes.

Yields: 6 servings

ROAST VENISON WITH BACON AND ONION

Venison, leg roast 4 lbs

Ingredients:

Olive oil
Fresh cracked black pepper 2 T
Onions, chopped fine 1 pt
Bacon 1 lb

Sauce:

Brown sauce 1 pt

Season roast with pepper and oil. Place onions in roasting pan with roast. Cover the roast with bacon slices and roast at high heat (400°F) for approximately 1 hour or until the internal temperature reaches 135°F. Remove bacon, let roast rest for 15 minutes. Chop bacon and with onions add to 1 pint of brown sauce. Bring to a boil, then skim off all the fat. Slice roast thin. Serve with sauce and brussel sprouts.

Yields: 8 servings

RACK OF VENISON WITH ROASTED GARLIC AND SUNDRIED TOMATO CRUST

Venison rack, (1 side)
Olive oil ¼ c
Salt and pepper to taste

Crust Ingredients:

Olive oil 2 T
Roasted garlic 2 bulbs
Sundried tomato, chopped 1 c
Parmesan cheese ½ c
Parsley 2 tsp

Sauce

Brown sauce with Madeira wine 1 pt

French a rack of venison by trimming all excess meat away from bones and trimming the membrane from the meat, or ask your butcher to process your frenched rack of venison. Dredge rack in oil and seasonings. Sear the meat in a sauté pan and let cool. Prepare crust by roasting garlic bulbs in olive oil for approximately 30 minutes in a 350°F oven. Remove garlic from skin. Place garlic, tomatoes, cheese, and oil in a food processor and pulse into a paste. Add parsley. Cover the seared meat with paste and roast for approximately 20 minutes. Serve with Madeira sauce along with sautéed spinach, spaghetti squash, and fresh baked tomatoes.

Yields: 4 servings

VENISON CHOPS WITH GORGONZOLA WRAPPED IN PHYLLO

Venison, chops (with bone) 16 ea

Ingredients:

Olive oil 2 T
Salt
White pepper
Gorgonzola cheese 8 oz
Phyllo dough 1 lb box
Butter, melted 4 oz

Rub chops with oil and seasonings. Sear meat in a sauté pan, remove, and let cool. Prepare the wrap by stacking two sheets of phyllo dough on the table, lightly brush with melted butter. Cut the phyllo dough into two even pieces, and place one half on top of the other making the stack 4 sheets thick. Top each venison chop with cheese. Wrap chops with Phyllo dough placing fold on the bottom. Brush with butter and place on baking sheet. Bake in a preheated 425°F oven until golden brown (approximately 10-15 minutes.) Serve with curried rice, glazed baby carrots, pearl onions, and steamed broccoli.

Yields: 8 servings

LOIN OF VENISON WITH BRANDY CREAM AND GREEN PEPPERCORNS

Venison, loin 2 lbs

Marinade:

Olive oil 2 T
Salt
White pepper

Sauce:

Green peppercorns 2 T
Dijon mustard 1 T
Brandy 4 oz
Brown sauce 1 c
Heavy cream 1 pt

Marinate loin with oil and seasonings. Pan roast the loin by browning the meat in a hot pan on the stovetop then finishing in the oven at 375°F for approximately 20 minutes. In a 2-qt saucepan, mash peppercorns, then add mustard and brandy. Flambé. Add brown sauce and heavy cream. Reduce by ½. Slice meat approximately ½-inch thick and serve with sauce. Garnish with green and yellow beans and sweet potato pancakes. Remember to serve meat rare. Well-done meat will be tough because of the loss of juices.

Yields: 6 servings

ROAST LEG OF VENISON WITH GARLIC AND ROSEMARY

Venison, leg roast 8-10 lbs
(bone-in)

Marinade:

Olive oil ½ c
Dijon mustard 1c
Fresh garlic, chopped 1c
Fresh rosemary, chopped ½ c

Rub leg with marinade. Refrigerate in marinade for 24 hours. Roast meat for 20 minutes in a 400°F oven, then lower heat to 350°F for approximately 1 hour. Remove when internal temperature reaches 125°F (use a meat thermometer). Wrap in foil and let set 20 minutes before slicing. Serve with roasted whole vegetables, steamed beans and brown sauce variation.

Yields: 8 servings

SAUTÉ

Sauté literally means *"to jump."* This dry heat cooking method uses a high heat and tender cuts of meat. The following steps need to be followed in order to ensure a tender tasty finished product.
- Use tender cuts from the loin and round.
- Cut the meat across the grain no thicker than ½-inch thick.
- Use a beveled or straight sided sauté pan. A cast iron skillet will also work because it will retain the heat.
- Start with a very hot pan.
- Add a small amount of oil.
- Lay the item away from you in the hot oil (not splashing on you).
- Let the meat cook until it loosens away from the pan.
- Shake the pan to loosen the meat.
- Turn the meat over only once.
- Remove meat from the pan when making sauce.

Note:
- Do not overload the pan. This will cool the pan and the meat will become tough, colorless and tasteless.
- Caramelize (brown) the meat for flavor and color.
- Prepare as close to service time as possible.

Venison, 2 lbs (sliced into medallions)
¼" x 2" round silver dollars

Marinade:

Olive oil ¼ c
Salt and pepper
Brown sugar ¼ c
Red wine vinegar ¼ c
Paprika 2 tsp
Onion, sliced 2 c
Dijon mustard ¼ c
Green peppercorns ¼ c

Sauce:

Brown sauce 1 pt

Marinate medallions for 2 hours. Sear meat in a sauté pan, remove and reserve. Deglaze with the remaining marinade and reduce by ½. Add brown sauce and let simmer. Add medallions back to sauce and serve with roasted red potatoes and glazed beets.

Yields: 6 servings

SAUTÉED MEDALLIONS OF VENISON
WITH APPLE CIDER SAUCE

Venison, 1 lb (sliced into medallions)
¼" x 2" round silver dollars

Marinade:

Apple Jack brandy ¼ c
Corn oil 2 T
Salt
Pepper

Sauce:

Cider vinegar 2 T
Apple cider 1 pt
Marinade from above
Basic brown sauce 1 c
Cinnamon stick 1 ea
Granny Smith apples peeled, cored, and sliced 3 ea

Marinate meat for 1 hour. Sear medallions in a hot sauté pan, remove and reserve. Deglaze pan with mixture of cider vinegar, apple cider and marinade. Reduce by ½. Add brown sauce and cinnamon stick and reduce by ½ again. Add apples and simmer for 10 minutes. Add reserved medallions, heat and serve with braised red cabbage and steamed potatoes.

Yields: 4 servings

SEARED VENISON TOSSED WITH BOW TIE PASTA AND TOMATOES

*Venison, 1 lb (sliced across the grain)
into ⅛" thick, 1" wide, 2" long pieces*

Marinade:

*Olive oil
Garlic 1 T
Salt and white pepper*

Sauce:

*Olive oil 1 T
Garlic 1 T
Onion, sliced 1 c
Zucchini, sliced 1 c
Yellow squash, sliced 1 c
Whole peeled tomatoes, canned 1lb, 12 oz*

Garnish:

*Fresh oregano
Fresh basil
Fresh cracked black pepper
Fresh grated Parmesan cheese
Multi-colored bow tie pasta 8 oz*

Marinate meat for 1 hour. In a sauté pan, sear meat at high heat, remove and reserve. Boil pasta, drain, and reserve. Prepare the sauce by sautéing garlic, onion, and squash. Add tomatoes and bring to a boil. Add reserved pasta and meat to the sauce. Garnish with chopped fresh herbs, pepper and grated cheese. Toss and serve immediately.

Yields: 4 servings

WISCONSIN STYLE VENISON WITH SOUR CREAM AND MUSHROOMS

Venison, 2 lbs (sliced across the grain)
into ⅛" thick, 1" wide, 2" long pieces

Ingredients:

Butter 2 oz
Mushrooms, sliced 1 lb
Onions, chopped ¼ c
White wine ¼ c
Cider vinegar 2 T
Ketchup 2 T
Beef broth 1 c

Flour ¼ c
Beef broth 1 c

Sour cream 1 c
Salt & white pepper

In a sauté pan, melt butter and sauté meat. Remove from pan and reserve. Sauté mushrooms, remove and reserve. Sauté onion, then add wine, vinegar, ketchup and 1 cup broth. Reduce liquid by ½. Combine flour and broth to make a white wash, add to the reduction, and season. Next add sour cream, but do **NOT** boil. Finish by adding reserved meat and mushrooms. Garnish with fresh chopped chives and serve over rice, pasta, or roasted potatoes.

Yields: 6 servings

Venison, 2 lbs (sliced into medallions)
¼" x 2" silver dollars

Marinade:

Olive oil 2 T
Cassis (black currant liquor) ¼ c

Sauce:

Sugar 2 T
Vinegar 2 T
Chicken broth 1/2 c
Brown sauce 1 c
Cassis 1/2 c

Marinate medallions for 1-2 hours. Sear meat in a sauté pan, remove, and reserve. Prepare the sauce by combining all the ingredients and bringing to a boil. Reduce by ½. Add meat and serve. Remember to serve meat rare. Well-done meat will be tough because of the loss of juices.

Yields: 6 servings

VENISON MEDALLIONS WITH PORT WINE AND CRANBERRIES

Venison, 2 lbs (sliced into medallions)
¼" x 2" round silver dollars

Marinade:

Olive oil
Salt and white pepper
Port wine ¼ c

Sauce:

Olive oil 1T
Onion, sliced 2 c
Dijon mustard 2 T
Sugar 2 T
Vinegar 2 T
Port wine 1 c

Garnish:

Whole cranberries ½ c
Water ½ c
Sugar ½ c

Brown sauce 1 pt

Marinate medallions for 1 hour. Cook the cranberries in the water and sugar until soft, and reserve. In a sauté pan, sear meat at high heat, remove and reserve. Prepare the sauce by combining all sauce ingredients, bringing to a boil and reducing to ½ cup. Add cooked cranberries, brown sauce, reserved meat and serve. Goes great with spaghetti squash and broccoli.

Yields: 6 servings

Venison Medallions with Apple Cider and Dried Currants

Venison, 2 lbs (sliced into medallions)
¼" x 2" round silver dollars

Marinade:

Brandy 1 c
Apple cider 1 pt
Dry currants 1 c
Ketchup ½ c

Sauce:

Brown sauce 1 pt

Marinate meat for 2 hours. Sear meat in a sauté pan, remove and reserve. Deglaze pan with remaining marinade. Flambé. Reduce by ½ and add brown sauce to adjust thickness. Add reserved meat and serve with scalloped potatoes and peas and carrots.

Yields: 6 servings

SEARED VENISON TOSSED IN A CAESAR SALAD
❖

Venison, 1 lb (sliced into medallions)
¼" x 2" round silver dollars

Marinade:

Olive oil 2 T
Salt and white pepper
Garlic, minced 2 T

Salad Dressing:

Fresh garlic, minced 1 T
Anchovies (optional) 4 ea
Olive oil 3 T
Dijon mustard 1 T
Eggs (optional) 2 ea
Parmesan cheese ½ c
Balsamic vinegar 1 T
Fresh cracked black peppercorn to taste

Salad:

Fresh Romaine lettuce 2 heads
Croutons 1 c
Tomato, wedges 8 ea
Fresh grated Parmesan cheese

Marinate medallions for 1 hour. Prepare greens by washing and removing core. To prepare the salad dressing, mash the garlic and anchovies into a paste, then add oil, mustard, and eggs. Mix well, then add cheese, vinegar, and pepper. Sear the venison in a sauté pan, and combine with the greens and dressing. Toss meat and garnish with tomato, croutons, and freshly grated cheese. Serve with vinegar and oil on the side

Yields: 4 servings

SAUTÉED MEDALLIONS OF VENISON
WITH YAKIMA APPLE SLAW

Venison, 1 lb (sliced into medallions)
¼" x 2" round silver dollars

Marinade:

Salt and white pepper
Apple Jack brandy ½ c

Apple Slaw:

Onion, thinly sliced ½ c
Apples, thinly sliced 2 c
Cabbage, shredded 1 c
Caraway seeds 1 T
Sugar 2 T
Apple cider vinegar 1 T
Apple Jack brandy 2 T

Sauce:

Brown sauce 1 pt

Marinate meat with the brandy and spices for approximately 2 hours. On the stovetop, heat brown sauce. Sear medallions in a sauté pan, remove and reserve. Deglaze the pan with brandy and flambé. Add onions, sauté lightly, and then add the remaining ingredients. Toss until wilted and soft. Serve the medallions on top of the Apple Slaw. Garnish with brown sauce.

Yields: 4 servings

VENISON MEDALLIONS WITH KAHLÚA RUM SAUCE

Venison, 2 lbs (sliced into medallions)
¼" x 2" silver dollars

Marinade:

Olive oil 2 T
Salt and pepper
Kahlua 2 T
Rum 2 T

Ingredients:

Onions, diced 1 T
Garlic, minced 1 tsp
Tomato concasser 1 c
Kahlúa ½ c
Rum ¼ c
Brown sauce 1 pt
Parsley, chopped 1 T

Marinate medallions for 1 hour. Sear meat in a sauté pan, remove and reserve. Prepare the sauce by sautéing garlic and onions, add tomatoes. Deglaze with Kahlúa and rum, (be careful—pour into a cup first then from the cup into the hot pan). Add brown sauce, parsley, and reserved meat. Serve with sautéed cabbage or pasta.

Yields: 6 servings

Venison With Plum Tomatoes And Basil

Venison, 1 lb (sliced across the grain)
into ⅛" thick, 1" wide, 2" long pieces

Sauce:

Olive oil 2 T
Onions, sliced ½ c
Garlic, minced 1 T
Plum tomatoes 1 qt
Fresh basil ¼ c
Fresh cracked black pepper

Sear meat in a sauté pan, remove and reserve. Sauté onions and garlic. Add tomatoes and reserved meat. Finish with fresh basil and cracked black pepper and serve with polenta or penne pasta.

Note: IF substituting dry basil use only 1 T

Yields: 4 servings

Venison Fajitas

Venison, 2 lbs (sliced across the grain)
into ⅛" thick, 1" wide, 2" long pieces

Marinade:

Olive oil ¼ c
Salt and pepper
Garlic, minced 1 T
Onion powder 2 tsp
Dry oregano 2 tsp
Cumin 1 tsp
Lime juice ¼ c
Jalpeño pepper, chopped 2 ea
Parsley, chopped 1 T
Beef broth ½ c

Vegetables:

Onions, sliced thin 2 ea
Green peppers, sliced thin 2 ea
Red peppers, sliced thin 2 ea
Fresh cilantro

Marinate meat overnight. Sear meat in a sauté pan, remove and reserve. Add vegetables, sauté, remove and reserve. Deglaze the pan with marinade and pour over sliced meat and vegetables. Finish with fresh cilantro and serve with warm tortillas, guacamole, and sour cream.

Yields: 6 servings

VENISON GYROS

*Venison, 2 lbs (sliced across the grain)
into ⅛" thick, 1" wide, 2" long pieces*

Marinade:

*Olive oil 2 T
Salt and pepper*

Vegetables:

*Red onions, sliced 1 c
Cucumbers, sliced 1 c
Tomatoes, sliced 1 c*

Cucumber Mint Sauce:

*Plain yogurt 1 pt
Mint, chopped 2 T
Green onions, chopped 2 T
Cucumber, peeled, seeded, minced ¼ c
Buttermilk ½ c*

8-10 Pita Bread

Marinate meat for 1 hour. Prepare the cucumber mint sauce by combining all ingredients. Slice vegetables and reserve. Sauté meat. Place meat, vegetables and sauce in pita pocket or roll in pita bread.

Yields: 6 servings

Stir-Fry is a fast cooking method using a wok or sauté pan. Venison can be used in an endless variety of stir-fried and oriental dishes. The meat should be cut thin, across the grain and tender for this method. It is best to use tender cuts from the loin and round.

- Cut the meat across the grain no thicker than ¼-inch thick.
- Use a wok or sauté pan.
- Start with a preheated and very hot pan.
- Season (coat) the hot pan with a small amount of sesame oil.
- Lay the item away from you in the hot oil (so as not to splash yourself).
- Let the meat cook away from the pan. By this I mean do not remove the pan from the heat. Shake the pan to loosen the meat.
- Brown (caramelize) the meat to enhance flavor and color.
- Do not overload the pan. This will prevent browning and will make the meat tough.
- Remove meat from the pan when making the sauce.
- Prepare as close to service time as possible.

VENISON WITH SNOW PEAS IN OYSTER SAUCE

*Venison, 1 lb (sliced across the grain)
into ⅛" thick, 1" wide, 2" long pieces*

Marinade:

*Ginger, minced 1 tsp
Garlic, minced 1 T
Green onion 3 T
Sesame oil 2 T*

Sauce:

*Chicken broth 1pt
Cornstarch 1 T
Oyster sauce 1 c*

*Snow peas ½ lb
Red pepper, large dice, 1 ea*

Marinate meat 1-2 hours. Mix cornstarch with chicken broth and reserve. Heat wok, add meat, sear and remove. Stir-fry red pepper and snow peas, add cornstarch mixture and oyster sauce to wok. Bring to boil and reduce to desired thickness. Return stir-fried meat to wok, blend, and serve over rice or steamed shredded cabbage seasoned with five-spice powder.

Yields: 4 servings

ORIENTAL NOODLES WITH SESAME VENISON

Venison, 1 lb (sliced across the grain)
into ⅛" thick, 1" wide, 2" long pieces

Marinade:

Ginger, minced 1 T
Garlic, minced 2 T
Green onion ¼ c
Sesame oil 2 T

Ingredients:

Toasted sesame seeds 1/4 c
Linguine 8 oz

Snow peas 4 oz
Oriental straw mushrooms, canned 16 oz
Soy sauce 3/4 c

Green onions, chopped ¼ c

Marinate meat 1-2 hours. Toast the sesame seeds and reserve. Cook linguine and reserve. Stir-fry venison in the wok, then add snow peas, drained mushrooms, and soy. Bring to a boil, then add linguine. Garnish with chopped green onions and sesame seeds.

Yields: 4 servings

Stir-Fry Venison With Broccoli and Garlic Sauce

Venison, 2 lbs (sliced across the grain)
into ⅛" thick, 1" wide, 2" long pieces

Marinade:

Soy sauce ¼ c
Sherry wine ¼ c
Sesame oil ¼ c

Ingredients:

Ginger, chopped 2 T
Garlic, chopped ¼ c
Green onions, chopped 1 bunch
Broccoli, blanched 1 bunch
Oriental dark sauce 3 c
Hoisin sauce 2 T

Marinate meat 1-2 hours. Prepare the Oriental Dark Sauce from sauce section of book. Blanch broccoli. Heat wok, then stir-fry ginger, garlic, green onions, and meat; remove and reserve. Add blanched broccoli and dark sauce, bring to boil. Return meat to sauce, adjust seasonings, and serve over rice or Chinese noodles.

Yields: 6 servings

Braising and Stewing

Braising and stewing are combination cooking methods used for less tender cuts of meat such as the leg, shoulder or neck. A combination cooking method starts out using dry heat, caramelizing or searing technique, then the addition of moisture (water or wine), lower temperatures, and longer cooking times which, if done properly, will turn tougher, drier meat cuts into sumptuous, fork-tender feasts. The following is an introduction to correct braising and stewing methods:

Braising
- Use less tender cuts such as the shoulder, neck or the round.
- Portion size 6-8 oz. or larger. Example—a pot roast, braised ribs or even the whole hind leg.
- Brown meat at high heat on all sides in a large skillet or roasting pan and deglaze with liquid. This means to add broth, wine or water and remove the browned juices that have stuck on the bottom of the pan. This adds flavor and color.
- Season, bring to a boil, cover and finish in the oven.
- The meat will be fork-tender when done.

Stewing
- Use less tender cuts such as the shoulder, neck or the round.
- Cut the meat into small cubes. Example—beef stew or ragout.
- Use a stewing pot or even a pressure cooker. Brown the meat first, then add vegetables and liquid; bring to boil, season, simmer until tender.
- Remember, do not overload the pan when adding the meat. This will prevent browning and make the meat sweat, thus making it tough.
- The meat will always be well-done and fork-tender when braising and stewing. Once the meat is cooked, you can season, strain and adjust the thickness of the sauce.

VENISON HUNTER STYLE

Venison, 2 lbs ('½" cubes)

Dredge:

Flour 1 c
Salt and pepper to taste
Garlic 1 T

Sauce:

Butter 2 T
Garlic, chopped 1 T
Onion, chopped 1 c
Mushrooms, quartered 8 oz
White wine ¼ c
Whole, peeled tomatoes, canned 1 lb, 12 oz
Brown sauce 1 pt
Parsley 1 T

Dredge meat in seasoned flour mixture. Brown meat in a sauté pan, remove and reserve in a casserole dish. In the same sauté pan, prepare the sauce, by sautéing garlic, onions, and mushrooms. Deglaze pan with wine. Add tomatoes, brown sauce and parsley; bring to boil. Pour sauce over meat, mix well, bake in preheated oven at 350° F for one hour. Serve with roasted potatoes and turnips.

Yields: 6 servings

VENISON AND BEAN STEW

Venison, 2 lbs (½" cubes)

Ingredients:

Beans (black, red or white) 1 lb
Water 1 qt

Garlic, minced ¼ c
Onion, diced 2 c
Smoked ham hock 2 ea
Whole peeled tomatoes, or stewed tomatoes, canned 1 lb, 12 oz
Chicken broth 1 qt
Bay leaf 3 ea
Thyme 1 tsp
Parsley 2 T
Fresh cracked black peppercorn 1 tsp
Fennel seed 1 tsp
Salt

Bread crumbs 2 c
Butter 4 oz

Soak the beans overnight. Drain the liquid and reserve beans. Brown the venison in a pan on the stovetop, remove and reserve. Sauté the garlic, onion, and ham hock. Add the tomatoes, broth and seasonings, mix well. Stir in the reserved meat and beans; bring to a boil. Place mixture in a casserole pan, top with bread crumbs mixed with butter and bake for approximately 2 hours. Serve with broccoli, cheese sauce, and pickled beets.

Yields: 6 servings

SHEEP CAMP STEW

Venison, 2 lbs ('½" cubes)

Marinade:
Madeira wine 8 oz

Ingredients:

Olive oil ½ c
Garlic, chopped 2 T
Onion, chopped 2 c
Carrots, diced 1 c
Celery, diced 1 c

Flour 1/2 c
Beef broth, 1 pt

Potatoes, diced 1 c
Stewed tomatoes, canned 1 lb, 12 oz
Beef broth 3 c
Mushrooms, quartered ½ c
McCormick Beef Stew Seasoning, 1 package

Marinate the meat in wine for 1 hour. In a deep pot, brown meat in oil. In the same deep pot, add garlic, onions, carrots, celery, and remaining marinade; sauté. Combine beef broth and flour making a white wash and add to the pot. Then add potatoes, tomatoes, broth, mushrooms, and seasonings. Simmer 1 hour.

Yields: 6 servings

Venison Shanks in Beer and Kraut

Venison shanks, 2 lbs (boned and tied)

Marinade:

Oil 2 T
Garlic powder 1 tsp
Salt and pepper

Vegetables:

Onions, large dice 1 c
Caraway 1 T
Paprika 1 T
Dijon mustard 2 T
Chicken broth 1 qt
Beer, can 12 oz
Red potatoes, small 2 lb
Sauerkraut 2 lb

Marinate the meat for 1-2 hours. On the stovetop, heat pan and brown meat. Add onions, spices, mustard, broth and beer, bring to a boil. Simmer for 1½ hours. Add potatoes and sauerkraut; simmer ½ hour more or until fork tender.

Yields: 6 servings

VENISON WITH PAPRIKA CREAM

Venison, 2 lbs (½" cubes)

Dredge:

Flour 1 c
Salt and pepper to taste
Garlic 1 T
Paprika 2 T

Sauce:

Butter 2 T
Onions, chopped ½ c
Flour 5 T
Paprika 1 T
Milk 1 c
Sour cream 1 c
Brown sauce 1 pt

Dredge meat in seasoned flour mixture. Brown meat in a sauté pan, remove and reserve into a casserole dish. Using the same pan, prepare the sauce by sautéing onions in butter, add flour and paprika, and lightly cook. Add milk and simmer until thick. Add sour cream and pour over meat in casserole dish. Bake in preheated 350° F oven, for one hour. Be careful not to boil as the sauce will separate. Serve with green and yellow beans and roasted new potatoes.

Yields: 6 servings

Venison and Wild Mushroom Ragout

Venison, 2 lbs ('/₂" cubes)

Ingredients:

Onions ½ c
Paprika 1 T
Garlic, minced 2 tsp
Button mushrooms, quartered ½ c
Shiitake mushrooms, quartered ½ c
Portabello mushrooms, large dice ½ c
Crimmini mushrooms, quartered ½ c
Sherry wine ½ c
Whole peeled plum tomatoes 1 c
Basic brown sauce 1 c
Salt and pepper

Sear meat in a saucepan, remove and reserve. Sauté onions, paprika, garlic, and mushrooms. Deglaze with wine. Add tomatoes and sauce then reserved meat. Bring to a boil and finish in oven at 350°F until meat is fork tender. Serve over buttered egg noodles.

Yields: 6 servings

VENISON IN GREEN CHILI STEW

Venison, 2 lbs ('/₂" cubes)

Marinade:

Olive oil 2 T
Onion, diced 1 c
Garlic, minced 1 T
Jalapeño chilies, chopped 2 ea
Whole, peeled tomatoes, canned 1 lb, 12oz
Green mild chilies, diced 12 oz can
Potatoes, large dice 1 lb
Chicken broth 1 qt
Cumin 2 tsp
Dry oregano 2 tsp
Salt and pepper

Sauté onion, garlic, and jalapeño chilies. Add meat, tomatoes, green chilies, potatoes and broth. Season with herbs and spices. Cook until tender. Adjust heat by varying the amount of chilies. Serve with sour cream, chips and a good tequila.

Yields: 6 servings

GROUND VENISON

Most people get their excess meat made into ground venison. Always remember to use only clean, good meat. Remove all tendons and hair. Use tough cuts from the shank, neck, shoulder and all trimmings. Mix with pork for added moisture. When grinding, use clean, cold equipment. Sanitation is extremely important because the meat will have more surface area exposed to air, cutting board, equipment and your hands.

When binding meats such as meatloaf or meatballs, use one egg per pound of meat. Use these meats as you would for all ground beef or lamb recipes, such as meatloaf, stuffed cabbage, meatballs and chili, or as sausages such as Italian sausage for lasagna or ravioli. Remember to ask your butcher for coarse grind if you like your chili chunky.

You may wrap or freeze the venison in large portions and grind at a later date when ready to prepare sausage or ground meat. Sausage and ground meat tend to get freezer burn quicker than if the meat was frozen in large cuts.

In some of the recipes, you can substitute pork butt or salt pork for pork belly. Eliminate any additional salt from the recipe when using salt pork.

GROUND VENISON MIX

Venison, 3 lbs
Pork butt, 1lb

Mixture:

Worcestershire sauce $^{1}/_{4}$ c
Whole eggs 4 ea
Salt 1 tsp
Pepper 1 tsp

Grind meat through large die of grinder. Add remaining ingredients and grind through medium die of grinder. Test sample by frying a small amount for tasting. This mix will be used as a base for other recipes such as stuffed eggplant, stuffed zucchini, stuffed peppers, or stuffed grape leaves. Also use this mixture for meatballs, meatloaf, and cabbage rolls, or any other dish that requires ground beef, lamb or pork.

Yields: 3-lb to 4-lb batch or 6 servings

HERBAL MEATLOAF

Ground venison mix, ½ recipe

Ingredients:

Onion, chopped fine ½ c
Green pepper, chopped fine ½ c
Parmesan cheese ¼ c
Garlic salt 1 T
Thyme ½ tsp
Basil ½ tsp
Parsley ½ tsp
Ketchup ¼ c

Sauté onions and green pepper, and let cool. Mix all the dry spices, then add ketchup, onion, and pepper to ground venison mix. Shape into a loaf. Bake at 350°F for 45 minutes. Serve with basic brown sauce and mashed potatoes.

Yields: 6 servings

Venison Taco Meat

Venison Mixture:

Venison, ground 2 lbs
Oil 2 T
Onion ¼ c
Onion powder ½ tsp
Chili powder 2 T
Cumin 2 T
Paprika 2 tsp
Salt and pepper to taste
Flour ¼ c
Beef broth 1 pt

In a saucepan, brown meat, add onions, spices and flour. Add broth and cook until desired thickness. Serve in a taco salad, or as hard and soft tacos, or as burritos filling.

Yields: 6 servings

SWEETWATER VENISON CHILI

Venison, coarse ground 2 lbs
Oil 2 T

Ingredients:

Onion, diced 1 c
Garlic, minced 2 T
Red peppers, diced 1 c
Green peppers, diced 1 c
Chili powder 2 T
Ground cumin 1 T
Paprika 2 tsp
Dry oregano 1 tsp
Cayenne pepper ½ tsp
Crushed tomatoes 1 pt
Brown sugar 2 T
Brown sauce 1 pt
Salt to taste
Fresh cracked black pepper ½ tsp

In a large pot, caramelize the meat. Add onions, garlic and peppers, then sauté. Mix spices and add to the mixture. After stirring, add tomatoes, brown sugar, and brown sauce. Simmer for 1 hour. Serve and garnish with sour cream and grated cheddar cheese.

Yields: 6 servings

Venison and Eggplant Casserole

Venison Mixture:
Venison, coarse ground 2 lbs
Olive oil 2 T
Garlic, minced 1 T
Onion, minced 1 c
Whole peeled tomatoes with juice 1 qt
Tomato paste 1 T
Cumin 1 tsp
Salt and pepper to taste
Parsley, chopped 1 T

Eggplant Mixture:
Eggplant, medium size, sliced ¼" thick 2 ea
Flour 1 c
Salt and pepper to taste

Béchamel Sauce:
Butter 3 T
Flour 3 T
Milk 1½ pt
Salt and pepper to taste
Nutmeg to taste
Egg yolks 3 each
Parmesan cheese 2 T

In a saucepan, prepare the béchamel sauce, by first melting the butter. Add flour, hot milk, and season. Mix egg yolks and cheese and add to mixture in saucepan. Reserve. Next, prepare the venison mixture by sautéing the meat and adding onions, garlic, and spices. Add tomatoes and simmer for 10 minutes. Reserve. Prepare the eggplant mixture; dredge eggplant in flour, pan fry, and set aside. Assemble the casserole starting with a layer of venison mixture, then eggplant, and top with béchamel. Bake in a preheated oven at 350°F for 1 hour.

Yields: 6 servings

Breakfast Style Venison Sausage

Venison, 3³/₄ lbs sliced into 1" strips
Fresh pork belly, 2 lbs sliced into 1" strips

Ingredients:

Salt 3 T
White pepper 2 tsp
Sage 1 T
Nutmeg 2 tsp
Thyme 2 tsp
Cayenne pepper 1 tsp
Ground ginger ½ tsp
Ice water 1 c

Mix spices and toss with meat. Add water and toss again. Grind meat through ¼-inch die. Mix well. Make into patties or stuff into hog casings for links. You may also store as bulk for various casserole dishes.

Yields: 6-lb batch

ONION SAUSAGE

Venison, 3³/₄ lbs sliced into 1" strips
Fresh pork belly, 2 lbs sliced into 1" strips

Ingredients:

Salt 3 T
Nutmeg 1 tsp
Sugar 2 tsp
Onions, chopped fine ¼ c
Fresh cracked black pepper 2 tsp
Ground marjoram 2 tsp
White pepper 1 tsp
White wine ¼ c
Onion powder 1 T

Mix spices and toss with meat. Add wine and toss again. Mix well and grind meat through ¼-inch die (twice). Make into patties or stuff into hog casings for links. You may also store this as bulk and use for lasagna or meat sauce and pizza.

Yields: 6-lb batch

SWEET ITALIAN SAUSAGE

Venison, 3³⁄₄ lbs sliced into 1" strips
Fresh pork belly, 2 lbs sliced into 1" strips

Ingredients:

Salt 3 T
Sugar 2 T
Fresh cracked black pepper 1 tsp
Red wine ¼ c
Fennel seed 2 tsp

Mix spices and toss with meat. Add wine and toss again. Grind meat through ¼-inch die (twice). Mix well. Make into patties or stuff into hog casings for links. You may also store as bulk and use for lasagna or meat sauce and pizza.

Yields: 6-lb batch

FRESH HOT ITALIAN SAUSAGE

Venison, 3³/₄ lbs sliced into 1" strips
Fresh pork belly, 2 lbs sliced into 1" strips

Ingredients:

Salt 3 T
Sugar 1 T
Dry hot pepper flakes 1 T
Ground coriander 1½ tsp
Caraway ¼ tsp
Fresh cracked black pepper 2 tsp
Red wine ¼ c
Fennel seeds 1½ tsp

Mix spices and toss with meat. Add wine and toss again. Mix well and grind meat through ¼-inch die (twice). Make into patties or stuff into hog casings for links. You may also store this as bulk and use for lasagna or meat sauce and pizza.

Yields: 6-lb batch

SAUCES, SPICE BLENDS AND RUBS

SAUCES

Sauces are the foundation to many of the recipes in this book. They can be made ahead and stored in the refrigerator for up to one week. The brown sauce can be frozen in small deli containers or in ziplock bags. Store bought jarred or canned brown sauces will work as well.

SPICE BLENDS AND RUBS

The recipes in this section include various spice blends and rubs that can be used for meats that are grilled and roasted. The dry spice blends or rubs can be made in advance and stored in an air-tight container away from heat and out of direct sunlight. They can be used on all types of cuts of meats and fish. The purpose of a rub or marinade is to develop flavor and act as a tenderizer. The rubs work by drying and breaking down the connective tissue.

BASIC BROWN SAUCE

Ingredients:

Olive oil
Onion, diced ½ ea
Carrot, diced 1 ea
Celery, diced 1 stick
Tomato paste ¼ c
Flour ½ c
Beef broth 48 oz
Bay leaf 1 ea

In a sauce pan, brown the onion, carrot and celery. Add the tomato paste and continue browning. Combine flour, broth and bay leaf and add mixture to browned vegetables. Simmer for 1 to 2 hours. Skim off impurities from top during simmering. Strain and store. This basic brown sauce is referred to throughout the book. It may be made in advance and stored in the freezer.

Yields: Approximately 1 quart

ORIENTAL DARK SAUCE

Ingredients:

Chicken broth 1 pt
Hoisin sauce 2 T
Soy sauce 2 T
Sugar 1 T
Ginger, chopped 1½ tsp
Green onion, chopped ¼ c

Corn starch 3 T
Chicken broth ½ c
Sherry wine 2 T

In a sauce pan, blend broth, hoisin, soy, sugar, ginger, and onion. Bring to a boil. Mix cornstarch with broth and wine, add to liquid in sauce pan. Simmer for 15 minutes, strain, and use. Note: this sauce can be made in advance, but cannot be frozen.

Yields: 3 cups

Venison Rib Rub

Ingredients:

Paprika $\frac{1}{2}$ c
Brown sugar $\frac{1}{2}$ c
Garlic powder 2 T
Onion powder 2 T
Black pepper $\frac{1}{4}$ c
White pepper 2 T
Dry mustard 1 T
Chili powder 1 tsp
Salt 2 T

Combine spices, rub ribs, and let cure for 24 to 48 hours. Broil or grill ribs with low heat. Serve with barbecue sauce.

Yields: Approximately 2 cups of spice blend, enough for two racks of ribs.

VENISON LEG RUB

Ingredients:

Olive oil
Shallots, minced 2 T
Garlic, minced 3 T
Onion powder 2 T
Chili powder 2 T
Paprika 1 T
Black pepper 1 tsp
Salt 1 T
Soy sauce ¼ c
Instant coffee 2 T
Water 2 T

Mix dry spices with shallots, garlic and oil. Mix instant coffee with liquids. Combine dry spice blend with the coffee mixture, rub on leg, let stand 24 hours. Roast at high heat, serve with brown or barbecue sauce variation.

Yields: Approximately ½ cup of dry ingredients, enough for one leg of venison

CAJUN SPICE BLEND

Ingredients:

Salt 4 T
Sugar 2 T
Thyme, ground 2 tsp
Onion powder 1 T
Paprika ½ c
Cayenne pepper 2 T
White pepper 1 tsp
Coriander, ground 2 tsp
Oregano, ground 2 tsp
Fennel seed 2 tsp
Cumin, ground 1 tsp

Combine all spices; rub meat with oil, then cover with spice blend. Let cure for 24 hours. Broil or grill with high heat. Use as a rub on ribs, blackened meats and fish, or as an ingredient in dishes such as bean stews, etc. To eliminate the fire hot, cut back on the cayenne and white pepper.

Yields: Approximately 1¼ cup, enough for approximately 6-lbs of venison

VENISON JAMAICAN JERK RUB

Ingredients:

Chili powder 1 T
Ground allspice ³/₄ tsp
Ground ginger ¼ tsp
Cayenne pepper ¼ tsp
Ground black pepper ¼ tsp
Salt ½ tsp
Olive oil 2 T

Combine all dry spices, rub meat with oil, then cover with spice blend.
Let stand 1 hour before grilling. Especially good on rack of venison.

Yields: Approximately 2 Tablespoons of dry ingredients, enough for two
pounds of venison

RED ONION MARMALADE

Ingredients:

Red onion, minced 1 lb
Red wine vinegar ½ c
Red wine ½ c
Maraschino cherry juice ½ c
Brown sugar ¼ c

Combine all ingredients and simmer for 1 hour. Use as barbecue sauce, accompaniment, or sauce for any game meat.

Yields: 1 pint

CACHE CREEK ENTERPRISES
INFORMATIONAL PAGE

❖

- *The Art of Cooking Venison* is a must for every hunting company.
- Great gift idea. Discount rate for orders of more than 10 books.
- Outfitters discount rates available.
- *The Art of Cooking Venison* is the first of a series of game cookbooks and videos. Soon to follow will be:
    - *The Art of Barbecuing and Grilling Game*
    - *The Art of Cooking Salmon*
    - *The Art of Cooking Small Game, Pheasant, Grouse, Rabbit, Quail and More*
- Chef Wutsch is available by request for special events, cooking demonstrations, speaking engagements, seminars, hunting and fishing camp chef.
- Cache Creek Enterprises also recruits employment opportunities and placement of chefs and cooks for camps and outfitters.

For more information please contact:
Albert Wutsch
Cache Creek Enterprises
PO Box 1374
Indiana, PA 15701
724-349-2067